RHAPSODY AND HUE

Poetry, Verse, Resonance
Volume: II

By

Roisin Rzeznik

RoRzeznik Publishing

Merton, Wisconsin

Rhapsody and Hue Writen by Roisin Rzeznik Published
by RoRzeznik Publishing
Merton, Wisconsin 53056

Roisin Rzeznik

© 2019 Roisin Rzeznik

RoisinRzeznik@yahoo.com

Cover photography by Roisin Rzeznik.

ISBN-13: 978-0-9892142-2-3

For Van Thanh Callies

An amazing man...fearless and loving, a dedicated and compassionate friend. God Bless you & keep you!
"My hero; my friend, love is forever."

TABLE OF CONTENTS

Rhapsody

Roisin Rzeznik

You and Me

Hue

RHAPSODY

RHAPSODY

I Need A Friend

Don't Need No Lies

Don't Need No Using

I Need You Baby

Throw Away That Pride

Help Roll Away This Stone

Humble Yourself

Get Down On Those Knees

I Need Somebody

Who Will Stay

Pray

Pray With Me

Please

Save The Day

Pray

Pray

Pray

DIAMOND IN THE ROUGH

This Is just the way it came to me

with you

And

Your heartfelt friendship...

On My Mind

Thank You,

Baby You Are

A Diamond In the Rough

Like A Magician

From The Mist You Emerge

Standing Tall

Time Stands Still

Shrouded In Mystery

I Can See From Here

Baby, Did I hear them say,

"You Ain't Ure"

No, No...

You're Magic

From a Dream

I Can See What You Got

Will You Baby

Give Me Baby

Give Me My Fill

Will You Give It To Me

Fill My Heart With What You've Got

Thrill Me Baby

Thrill Me Baby

I Know You Got A Lot

Show Me The Truth In It All

Show Me Your Masterpiece

Baby, I Know What You've Got

I Feel You Moving Closer

Baby, Why Are You Holding It In

I Feel You

Moving Closer Baby

I Want to heal you

Your Voice Came Calling On The Wind

Didn't Think I Needed Anyone

I Think You Think You Need

But Baby You're Everything To Me

Look A Little Closer

I Know You're Mine

Show Me the Truth in it All

Whisper It On The Wind

Show Me Your Masterpiece

Baby I Know What You've Got

Breathe Deep-Just Let It

Let It All In

Will You Baby

Give Me Baby

Give Me My Fill

Will You Give It To Me

Fill My Heart With What You Got

Thrill Me Baby

Thrill Me Baby

I Know You Got A Lot

Show Me The Truth In It All

Show Me Your Masterpiece

Baby, I Know

I know, What You've Got

I Know You Got A Lot

Will You Baby...

Show Me The Truth In It All

Show Me

Your Materpiece

A RARE BIT OF HONESTY

A Rare Bit Of Honesty
For A Friend
I'm Trapped
In What Should Have Been A Dream
Alone And Scared
I Never Know Who's On My Side
Beside Myself
Is Where I Sit
In This Nightmare Called The Dream
I Heard You Scream
I Heard You Scream
I Was Afraid Your Foot Was In Their Net
Then I Heard You Scream,
"Put That Cat Back!"
You're Screaming, "Put The Cat Back!"
I Hear You Scream
In This Nightmare

Maybe You Don't Know...
Honesty When You Hear It

When You Ask, "Are You Holding On"

But Dear, It's Loud And Clear

"Ratta-tat-tat"

When You Scream, "Put The Cat Back!"

You're Sure Of It

"Ratta-tat-tat!"

You Know, I'm Through

Through With It

Through With it All

"Put It Back!"

"Ratta-tat-tat!"

"Put It Back!"

I Heard You Screaming, So Sure Of It!

No, cure for it

It Should Have Been A Dream

It's A Nightmare

"Ratta-tat-tat"

I'm Trapped

By The Tom Cat

Alone And Scared

I hear you Scream

Top Cat's Not The Tom Cat

He's A Lion.

I'm Sure

I'm Reaching For You

Now What Are You Going To Do

You Want To Know

"Are You Holding On"

You're Going To Get Trapped

In This Nightmare Too

I Love You Babe For Stepping In

I Put It Back

"Ratta-tat-tat"

To Save Your Soul

Because You Were Reaching In

The Top Cat's Down For The Moment

Now You Know Why,

I Walk Alone

I Heard You Scream

Because You Were Reaching In

I'm Not Going To Fold

Because You Mean Something To Me Dear

You're In This Atmosphere

As I Walk Alone.

I Want Us To Get Old

Linger Dear

Linger...

Now

"Ratta-tat-tat"

Now

Wear Your Medal Of Gold

Let's End The Nightmare

So The Dream Can Begin

So The Dream Can Unfold

I Put It Back

"Ratta-tat-tat

I'm Ready For You

Are You Going To Let Me In

"Ratta-tat-tat

I Put It Back

So You Could Win

The Cat With the Chesire Grin

YOU

I Wanna Know

I Wanna Know

You

Are You The One

I've Spent These Days

Of

Solitude

Thinking About You

Dreaming

Of

You

I Feel Your Heart

Am I All Wrong

I Feel You There

You Make Me Stronger

I Wonder…

Do You Know…

What You Mean To Me

Do You Know…

How Much I Care

Where You've Been

Doesn't Matter To Me

Why Should It Matter To Me

It Doesn't Matter Anymore

As Long As You Love Me

As Long As You Are There

As Long As You Don't

Leave Me Standing Here

All Alone

Now That I Know

I Need You

Let Me Know You're There

Now That I Know

I Need You

Let Me Know You're There

FOR YOU

I Will Carry You
Know That You Are Loved
…Every Moment Of Every Day
Sleep Through The Night
I Feel Your Pain
When I'm Not Sure…
He Whispers to Me Your Name
Even On Nights Such As These
I Will Carry You
You're Not Alone
I'm Beside You On My Knees
If You Slow And Breathe Deeply
Eyes Closed Tight,
Reach
I'll Take Your Hand While You Sleep
Breathe Deeply
You Are Loved

KNOW

You Don't Really Want To Know
I'm Sitting Here
Peering At My Wounds
I Think, If You Saw Them...
You'd Cry The Blues
Though I'd Never Know...
In Time, Stitches Will Be Removed
The Pain Is Almost Gone
All That Will Remain Are Scars
Our Scars
A Memory In Time, If You Didn't Know...
You'd Never Know...
The Wounds Inside Don't Heal That Quick
Hidden So Deeply Do They Ever Heal
No One Knows I Cry The Blues; For Me-For You
They Don't Understand Our Skin Really Is Thick
They'll Never Know What We Know...
Thanks Be To God That He Never Leaves Us Alone

POEM FOR DAVID

Human Hearts So Often Break

Some Love

Like Green Grass

In Winter Fades To Brown

Or Burns Quickly

Like Lightning From A Storm

There Is No Way To Explain

But Like The Green Grass Of Spring

Some Love

Is Made To Rejuvenate

CATWALK

A Divine Mosaic

A "Sequins" Of Events

Deo Gratias

It's Crystal Clear

The Reason Why

I Want You In My Life

The Writing Is On The Wall

It Has Been Written In Stone

This Was Set In Time

By A Hand Far Greater Than My Own

It's A Beautiful Dance

One We Cannot Deny

One We Cannot Avoid

A Purpose Unknown

Closing The Distance

Between You And I

I Know These Thoughts

These Feelings

Sweeter Than The Deodar

Sacred

My Heart Continues Praising

I Know Who You Are

Sacred

I've Felt This Magic In A Dream

Before Me Your Face

Amazing

Deo Volente

You Are My...

CHOSEN

I Want To Hear It

Tell Me You've Chosen

Closing My Eyes

Waves Crash Against The Wall

If I Dream Louder

Can I Make You Appear

Amid The Roar

I Hear Your Voice

As I Reach Out

I Stretch My Arms Wide

Standing Here, I Am Ready To Embrace You

I Know You've Chosen

Now I Disappear

The Cold Spray Drenches Me

If I Wish Harder Will I Feel You

I Want To Be Near You

Rescue Me From Living On The Edge

Define Me Beyond The Fray

The Drum Is Still Beating Out Of Time

Before They Extinguish My Light

If I Pray Long Enough

Will It Make Everything All Right

Chosen One

Will You Save Me Now

Before The Morning Light

I Know You've Chosen

MAHOGANY

Mahogany You Are One With Me Again

We Suffer The Same Experience

Time And Time Again

I Can Hear The Way You Purse Your Lips

The Rise And Fall

They Echo In The Storm

It Is As If I Can Reach Out

And Touch Them With My Fingertips

The Warrior's Song Is In Your Soul

You Guide Me Home Again

As Subtle As The Tones

Of Mahogany Running Through Your Hair

You See Through Me

Straight Down To My Soul

I Hear It In Your Song

You Never Told Them My Name

Your Eyes Penetrating My Heart Again

Where Do We Begin

The Wind Is Crying

As The Sky Drops Its Tears To The Ground

I Am So Lonely; When Do We Begin

I See Your Love For Me

It Is Reflected There in Your Eyes

You Give Me Direction Allowing Me To See

As Subtle As The Monogamy That Protects Your Soul

The Rain Is Falling On The Ground

It Plays Out Of Rhythm

Outside Of Time

I Close My Eyes I Hear The Sound

As You Purse Your Lips Again

You Give Me Strength To Carry On

You See Beyond What The World Sees In Me

Oh Mahogany,

Tear Away The Walls And The Chains That Bind This Lonely Heart

I Have Faith In Your Song

Like A Flame Your Soul Dances With Strength And Majesty

I Want To Be Consumed By Your Holy Heart

Your Love For Me Deeper Than The Arabian Sea

Open The Doors To This Old Heart

It Is So Scared To Love

I Am So Lonely Without You

Be The Love That Lights My Eyes Again

Restore My Soul

LAST NIGHT

I Feel Like I've Been Waiting

Waiting So Long

For You To Catch Up To Me

For You To Wake Up

For You To Finally See

For You To Hear My Song

When I Walked Away

I Thought You'd Follow

When It Should Be Easier Now

It Has Become A Deeper Misery

It Gets Harder And Harder Every Day

Loving You

It Doesn't Get Easier

The Price Only Steeper To Pay

It's Only Easier Now To Paint The Target On My Own Head

Right Above My Eyes

They'd Be Doing Me A Favor Then

My Pain Gone

I Know

_If I Go_

They'll Never See The Light Of Day

Before My Body Is Cold

They'll Be Wishing They Were Dead

And You'll Be Free To Leave The Game

I Will Never Leave It Without You

I Jumped In For You

With No Regret, No Retreat, And No Compromise

I've Seen The Love You Have In Your Eyes

Was This A Love Never Meant To Be

Last Night I Could Feel Your Pain

My Soul Cried

It Cried Out In Horror Screaming Your Name

In That Moment The Hardest Part Is Not Knowing

Are You Dead, Alive,

Or Are You Laying On The Ground Fighting To Survive

Each Time It's Like Dying Again

Tell Me It's Not All In Vain

This Choice I Made

For Love To Remain

Can't You Feel Me

Like I Feel You

Can't You Hear My Soul Calling Out Your Name

When Will You Walk Down This Road

It Leads You From Destruction

I Thought Our Love Was True

I Thought You'd Come To Me

I Hate This Game

There Is No One To Comfort Me
There Is No One To Carry My Pain
Who Is Willing To Comfort Me
To This Pain I Can't See An End
Sitting Here Sobbing Once Again
Tormented
And Then...
Outside My Window I Could See Him
In The Morning Light
Bravely He Came And Sat
With A Song In His Heart Just For Me
Ruffled Feathers For A Hat
A Bold And Beautiful Blue Jay
He Was Begging Me To Finally See
He Has Come To Comfort Me

COPAL-CEDAR AND ROSE-JASMINE

I Walk The Moonlit Path
Until I'm In Your Presence
Through The Woods
To The Center Of Your Universe
I'm With You Tonight
God Has Forgiven Our Trespasses
Beside The Brook
Among The Grasses
My Hand On Your Face
My Body Across Your Knees
My Head Resting In Your Arms
I Feel Your Grace
Your Touch Leaves Me Gasping
Beautifully Restless
As Comforting As An Eternal Sleep
Ambient Silver Dances
To The Rhythms Of The Water
And The Quiet Deep
Surrounded By Nature's Rites

Silently You Hold Me

In Tranquilities Care
My Senses Are Heightened
Your Hand Smoothing My Hair
In The Stillness
I Feel Your Love Seeping Into My Soul
Your Hand On My Cheek
A Soothing Aloe
Whispers Begin
Like A Mountain Breeze
Coaxing Me From Sleep
Your Fingers Follow The Lines Of My Face
I Feel A Love Pure Enough To Keep
Around Us
The Quiet Calls And Enchanting Songs
Of Many Creatures Unseen
The Darkness Of The Forest Is Liberating
Its Floor Dank Yet Serene
Its Secrets Filling My Head With Wonder
Your Scent Touches My Skin

Patchouli; Copal-Cedar And Rose-Jasmine
Caressing
I Remember Why I Came

The Velvet Night Reaches Above Us For Miles

Infinity Is Numbered

By The Stars

Heaven Is In Your Eyes

I Can See By The Light Of Your Smile

I Whisper Your Name

It Travels Forever In The Stillness

I Feel The Tears Drop From Your Eyes

Falling Upon My Face

Your Comforting Touch Takes Me Home

I Wake Again Without You

Just A Memory

NOW

Come Open The Floodgates
Let The Living Waters Flow
You Can Help Me Relate
Show Me Your Ways
The Angels Are Weary
All These Sacred Oils
Still Haven't Healed Me
Reach For Me Now
Let The Living Waters Flow
You Can Help Me Relate
Consecrate Your Child
Israel Is So Faraway
I've Had My Fill Of Twisted Fate
Yahweh
Come Open The Floodgates

OICHE SHAMHNA
-Samhain-

(Sov-In)

In That Familiar Place;

Where I Was Last Alone.

His Angel

Lighting Candles

With Prayers Of Hope And Song.

I Left It There With Him-The Talisman; All Alone.

A Song Of Joy In His Heart

In Passing, A Blessing,

His Hand Upon My Brow.

Returning Now,

My Face In Hands.

Internal Screams Of Desperation.

I Transcend

To A Place Of Peace

Alone.

In Communion,
Myself And My Lord.
All Became Still
Upon That Holy Hill
The Ancient Stained Glass
Spoke Its Truths.
Protected By God
Hidden In His Pavilion;
Held By Love
Enfolded Within His Dimension
Without Dominion
An Inaccessible Plane.
My Soul Painfully Cold
Fever
Rising Within Me.
Attacked With Force;

The Wind Struck From Behind.
Evil Railed Against The Tower.
Horrifying Protest Ensued,
A Tempest Wailed,

Objections;

I Remained.

The Devil Violently Enraged.

A Perch For Love,

Upon That Holy Hill.

Climaxing Prayers,

Angels Sung In Choir.

Warmth Within,

All Around Me

Sweet Fragrance

His Hand Upon Me.

It Was You I Saw There.

My Breath Allowed To Resume.

Eyes Opened.

WHY

How Do You Know

When You're So Faraway

How Can You Tell

If You've Found The Way

A Need To Know

The Word

Next To Me

I Keep It On My Bed

Open To The Pages

Where I Like To Lay My Head

I Know

The Answers Are All Here

But It Helps

To Hear It From A Friend

Do You Feel It Too

When I'm Dreaming

Can I Tell You

What You Already Know

What You've Already Read

Dreaming Of You

Leaves Me Needing

Bleeding Inside

Something We Both Hide

Aching For A Way

Can I Tell You

What You Already Know

What You've Already Read

Do You Feel It Too

When I'm Dreaming Of You

I Want To Feel

Feel

Your Sincerity

Hear It In Your Words

Then I Know

I Know I'm Not Alone

Can I Tell You

What You Already Know

To Know

To Know I'm Not Alone

To See

To See The Things I Cannot

How Do You Know

When You're So Faraway

How Can You Tell

If You've Found

The Way

A Need To Know

What You Already Know

From a distance
The best way to learn
A place to see the truth
Where façade disappears
True intentions are revealed

ATLAS

The Sign Say

I Don't Belong

Can You

Feel Free

Where You Don't

Belong

The Sign Say

Don't Walk

I Walk For Miles

The City

Will It

Embrace Me

Will It

Erase Me

Will It

Know Where to Call Home

I Know, Baybee, I Know

Even Angels Get Confused

Street Fights

Flashing Lights

Solitude Is Nowhere

I Want To Hide Away

In Your Arms

Where You Are

Is Where I Begin

The Maps Say

You're So Faraway

Baybee,

Does That Road

To Your Heart

Still Exist

Is It Nowhere

Painting For Hours

All Night-

Thoughts Of You Persist

Is It All Right

To Love You

From Afar

Baybee,

I Insist

My Love Is Nowhere Too

The Sun Set

Blue

Purple

Thoughts Of You

Reds Of Every Hue

And More Thoughts Of You

I Know, Baybee I Know

Nowhere

But Even Angels Need A Muse

Where You Are

Is Where I Begin

Nowhere

Looking Up

At The Stars Tonight

I Feel Your Love

Wrapping Around Me

As You Take Flight

Please Tell Me

The City Lights

Haven't Washed Away

Your Starlight

Tonight

Baybee,

Nowhere

Please Tell Me...

WHERE ARE YOU...

Tonight, I'm Just A Woman
Thinking About A Man
In A Dark Room
Where A Faint Glow
Is Light Enough To Write By
Outside
The Storm Grows
Louder...
Sleep Still Hasn't Come
The Wind Blows Stronger
As It Wrestles With Itself
I'm Feeling Quite Numb
I Rest My Face On The Glass
The Light Flashes In My Eyes
I Feel For A Moment
What It's Like To Be Alive
The Trembling Fades
It's Absorbed Into The Cool Glass
I Close My Eyes
And Press My Head Against the Pane
Thinking Of You

I Think I Can Feel Your Pain
You're As Faraway As...
And More Distant Than
The Flash
I Touch My Fingers To The Glass
Gently Tracing The Beads
Are They Your Tears
Falling From My Eyes
Light Still Flashing...
The Sparks
Reveal The Colors In Your Tears
Closing My Eyes Now
I Think I Can Hear You Breathing
Maybe Tonight
We'll Both...

A DIFFERENT CUP

Plastic Slides

And Limousines

Sugar Highs

And Magazines

Love Without A Thought

What Else Have You Bought

A Ticket To Ride

The Merry-Go-Round

Ever Spinning

So You Can Move Inside Life's Womb

Without Touching The Ground

Tempted By

A New High

As You Walk Into My Room

Will You Ever Really Let Me In

Which One Of Us

Is Willing

To Give Our Ticket Up

If We Love So Much

Why Are We

Spinning

Both Screaming

Let Me Off…

Ready To Drink

From A Different Cup

IN YOUR ARMS

In Your Arms

Do You Think

I Can Heal You

Do You Think

You Can

Do The Same

I Wonder If You Touch Me

Will What I Feel Remain

Will You Remain

If You Touch Me

Will What You Feel Be The Same

Do You Think

You Can Heal Me

Do You Think

I Can

Do The Same

WALK AWAY

Advice For A Friend

Walk Away

Walk Away

Is What My Conscience Says

Walk Away

Before You Care

My Advice to You

When All I Really Want Is to Rollover

And See You There...

TONIGHT

I miserable

there is not enough

Irish whiskey

in the world

to drive the loneliness from my soul

the walls are closing in

on the lies of happiness

the walls that haven't already crumbled

tonight it's hard to be a Christian

surrounded by politics

and

even more hypocrites

it's hard not to be in control

it's hard to have faith

prayer doesn't always come easy

it doesn't always protect from hate

it's hard to trust

In what I can't see

tonight it's hard to be good

and not just be in it for me

it's hard to see the future

it's hard to see the light

it's hard

so hard to be still and know…

Everything is going to be alright

when I'm choking on regret

that I've stored for years

I'm angry

there is no one to be angry with

I think I hate…

you watching me walk away

for not saving me…

Time and time again

for letting me throw it all away

then

now

for not being real

for taking my friend

for leaving me with…

No one else

alone to carry the pain

and there's no one to wipe the tears

there is no one to blame

for this sea of endless pain

for my wasted years…

There is no way out

without

The choices I have made

I scream for fairness

but it's never been

I scream for justice

but it feels at a loss

my friend

I've been cut off

it's all been taken away

again

and again

and again

for needing...

Love and affection

for not wanting to go with the flow

for not being someone I'm not

for not settling

for not being silent

for not letting go

I scream for love

its eyes are vacant

Its kiss...

Resides with someone else

its heart and arms are absent

it's blind and deaf

straight through to the core

a soul no more

it sings its own sad song

I know

it's not him

not anymore

it proclaims it's done nothing wrong

it watches me as I choke some more

tonight

if I could I'd run from everything

even though…

It would be better to choke even more

The only place I'll run tonight is

into the arms of my Savior

as I lay myself down

on the cold floor

and choke some more

I know

the whiskey only adds flavor

to a bitter pill

And the cold sad truth

It's hard to be a Christian

but somehow

the light always

returns

I know

I won't be alone

as I choke some more

at least

this way

I know

I'm alive

the loneliness burns

Inside

it's worse than before

THE VISAGE

I saw you

in the crowd

when he turned around

he had your face

I looked away

I looked around

then I looked again

to see you

look away

when he turned towards me

he had his own

again

the visage had changed

WHERE DREAMS COLLIDE

the sun's glare

cuts through

the cool air

it warms as it

slightly blinds;

the gulls dance

as they soar

above the highway ribbon

and the rhymes

PLATFORM PLEASANTRY UNAWARE

ascending

I feel you first

then I see you appear

watching from a distance

I see your form outlined

against the sky

distant from everyone near

what is that

I feel in the air

I'm too far away to scream

I can only raise my hand

with a sign

as I see you standing there

then you disappear

I come closer

I come to you

you're nowhere to be found

I wait...

But I'm not part of this forest

I'm not a tree

I -

I could never be

I leave
but not without a promise
between you and me
something we share
I hope next time
you'll see… Me
standing there
writing these lines
to tell you how much
I care
back at a distance
you re-emerge
hiding my tears
I watch you
ascending the stairs
wrapped in a cloak
High and serene
looking out from your watchtower
what a dream…

If you'd be looking for me
I'd run into your arms
you carry yourself
like royalty

havingjust steppedfrom a dream

stepping back through

from where you came

I watch you again

as you show the world

your specialflair

that's why I came

to see you

shine again

I count myself privileged

to be among

the many

even

the mice and men

NOTHING BUT YOU

I don't believe in wishes

I don't believe in dreams come true

I find myself believing in nothing

nothing but you

maybe you were heaven sent

in an altered state

Roisin Rzeznik

wrapped in a prayer

carried by a dream

I know you're there

you make me feel

even when I wouldn't

I see you

reflected in my eyes

you cover me

even when you shouldn't

I feel your light

you make it all look simple

I see now

it's true

nothing but you

I don't believe in wishes

I don't believe in dreams come true

I find myself believing in nothing

nothing but you

there is no one

like you

you're the kind

I've dreamt about

the kind

I know doesn't exist…

I see you now even when I shouldn't

wherever I go

you make me want to believe

I hear myself saying

it's true

tell me are you all show

do you believe

have you ever let go

nothing but you

I don't believe in wishes

I don't believe in dreams come true

I find myself believing in nothing

nothing but you

THE BUTTERFLY

greens and purples

Clover and thistle in Bloom

orange

on a butterfly's back

I watch

as its wings flutter

in unison

feeling for what's before it

with tiny hands and little knees

dancing a pirouette

will it take flight

what does it see

through those blackened eyes

does it know

if it's day or night

does it have a heart

instincts

a soul

does it know

if everything will be alright

does it pray

when it's on its knees

before it takes flight

does it feel dread

or impending doom

if it knew the facts

would it fear

does it even care

where it would land

if the winds would

either cease or begin

to blow…

Does it know

it's painted orange on black

from head to toe

as it takes flight

as it flies towards the trees

does it know

it's airborne

does it know

it would be safer on its knees

does it even care

does it see the forest for the trees

what does it know

Roisin Rzeznik

Embellishments of Evidence
Crystal Clear
Running in fear
I hold my breath
Avoiding premature death

KNIGHT OF SOUL

closing my eyes

I lay here…

Wide awake

waiting for my heart to un-brake

your voice filling my ears

washing away:

the years; the pain

the ghosts; the fears

…You have something I need…

It always feels like forever before sleep comes

before you come and take my hand

you sweep me off to sleep

like being swept off my feet

to a magic land;

to the safety of your kingdom

saving me from another disaster…

Pink alleyways with broken fire escapes

Spiders from Mars… And…

Bugs bigger than my face

you're saving me…

From the endless spiral staircase

and the bottomless bloody floor drains

like a magician or a physician of heart;

Amazing Grace

a Knight of Soul
bathing me in some sacred oil
taken from a golden bowl
save me once again
I'm closing my eyes to pretend
you're here with me
can you hear me
real to me
heal me - shield me
You're my rock; my soul
shield me
you're real to me
take my hand
so I don't fall
as you sweep me off to sleep
in your faraway land
once again
with you, My Rock; My Soul
you're saving me...
Knight of Soul

CERCA TROVA

CERCA TROVA...You are my Hero...
I see your face
when I dream
I see your face
I hear you scream
I scream your name
screaming it out–
the mental fallout
scream it out–
the mental fallout
I feel the pain
the pain you hide
the loneliness you mask
with all the bravado— pride
all the pain you've stored
it's angst piled up inside
let me love you
like friends do
let me hold your hand
while you–
scream!
Scream it out–
the mental fallout
scream it out–

the mental fallout

release it

release it

I'll chase the monsters away

that cause you harm,

they haunt you night and day

I want to hold you in my arms

release it

release the pain

scream it out! Scream it out!

Release your-Self

put your head in my lap

Babe...

Let me cradle your face in my hands

let my fingers touch your face

I'll brush the hair from your eyes

Let me wipe all those tears away

Babe...

I'm ready

to wipe those tears away

it's your pain I want to erase

scream it out-

the mental fallout

scream it out-

the mental fallout

put your mind at ease

let's join hands

become whole again

let's scream it out!!!

Let's scream it out!!!

Babe, you're the one

I want to embrace

let's scream it out!!!

Scream it out—

the mental fallout

scream it out—

the mental fallout

it's what hold you down

scream it out—

the mental fallout

with all your heart, Just…

"SCREAM-IT-OUT!"

IN THE SPOTLIGHT

Told to perceive it…

A misunderstanding

The only truth I perceive…

Underneath that Misunderstanding

Lives a desperate pain

A hard truth

A harsh realm of reality

Where tenderness

Can't be replaced

Where innocence

No longer lives

Somewhere between

Broken Dreams

And

An apology that's never spoken

Acceptance

Where we never quite belong

A lifelong fight to be recognized

For whom we are

Even though our hands are clean

They only point out what we've done wrong

How certain they are we don't belong

A longing to be fulfilled

A desire to stay

Yet we are still turned away

Short of being home

A place

Where even a Savior

Feels lost and alone

For even this martyr

Has nowhere to call home

For a prophet they don't see

Not in you

Not in He

We don't belong

On the very streets

Where we have grown

Aimlessly they continue

Aimlessly they roam

This concludes our lesson in complete ignorance

The spotlight we shine on stupidity

Or so it would seem

Yet nobody sees

But I know, I hear you, I feel you

As you scream…

"Here I stand alone!!!"

Roisin Rzeznik

Is it any consolation to know…

"Here we stand alone!"

Surrounded by the ignorance

Oh how it has grown…

But they say it'll be okay

They have enough for the entire town

Blinders in all shapes and sizes

Plenty to go around

A special pair set aside for you and me

They tell us it will protect us till we're full-grown

They say, "There are some dangers in loving freely."

The dangers of people that play games

Underneath the so called misunderstanding

Lives a desperate pain

A hard truth

A harsh realm of reality

"Baby, they don't even hear us scream.

They don't even know our names…

I am so lonely without you!"

This concludes our lesson in complete ignorance

The spotlight we shine on stupidity

Or so it would seem

Yet nobody sees

But I know, I hear you, I feel you

As you scream…

"Here I stand alone!!!"

I'm screaming…

"Here I stand to love you freely!"

"Here we stand alone!"

Take your blinders off, Baby we are full-grown…

"Here I stand to love you freely!"

"Here we stand alone!"

Roisin Rzeznik

THE LONE STAR

There are a million shooting stars tonight;
but only one lone star to make my life bright...

Would you want me there
If I could get to you
Somehow

Tell me
Am I getting to you
Like you're getting to me

Do you want to get to me
Like I want to get to you
Somehow

Tell me
You want to find a way
Tell me
You feel it too
Tell me you want this too
I watch from above
In black and white
I imagine it's you there tonight

I want to hold you so tight

Both of us down there
In black and white

Baby, I just want to
I just wanna be
In your arms...tonight

I don't want you to be cold
I don't want you to be alone
Won't you make my heart your home

What is this I feel with you
What is this I feel tonight
Are you feeling it too
Tell me

You want to find a way
Tell me
In black and white
Tell me You want me...in your arms tonight

Roisin Rzeznik

YOU ARE…

I'd ask you to love me

But I know you can't

A catch 22

That I would fall in love with you

After all this time

I find the one

The one;

Who can take away the pain

I found him in you

And I'll never be the same

I never thought

There'd come a day

When I would say

This to anyone…

I never thought I'd fall in love with you

I never thought I could really love anyone

Standing before you

I already know…

I'd beg for your hands to touch me

And your arms

To never let me go.

But the truth I know…

As you stand before me

For you, it can not be

I'd ask you to love me

But I know you can't

If there comes a day

When you are free

To love all of me

As free as I truly am

In love with you...

Please forget me not.

It is my own fault

You see

For being a fool

For waiting so long

It's fair

Now, I can finally see...

I can see, I should have to look at you

From here

Just close enough...

To see you

Yet far enough

To keep you from harm

Is this where we belong

Can you see

Where it all went wrong

The answer will make us strong

For now...

Presuming you feel the same

Wander not far from me

And I'll keep praying in Jesus' name

That you make your way into my arms

Because we really are the same

For if you ever come to me

You will never hear I can't

There will always be a way

Because I do

I've already fallen deeply in love

With you

I'd ask you to love me

But I know you can't

A catch 22

That I would fall in love with you

YOU AND ME

On this day

For you

A poem,

I did not write.

Instead

I thought on...

Hamlet's ramblings

And Lear's rages

And You

A great tragedy

Upon A hundred thousand

Of my pages

And Me

Closing my eyes against the pain

Praying for you.

Praying for one to come and make it alright.

Praying again

And again and again

For Him to come

For Him to make everything alright...

On this day

For you

A poem,

Roisin Rzeznik

I did not write.

Instead

I thought on...

Him

And wrote this

And another

For Van Callies

Tonight...

HUE

LOVE

Lord, let me live
Like You want me to live
Lord, let me love
Like You want me to love
Lord-Lord-Lord
Lord- In Heaven
Shine your loving grace on me
Shine your light in my life
Shine light on me
Fill my heart
Fill my life
Fill my soul
Shine your light
Make me whole

Lord, let me live

Like You want me to live

Lord, let me love

Like You want me to love

Lord let me love-let me love

Let me know your love

Lord! Let me Love!

Let me love like you love!

Love, let me love

Let me love

Let me love

Let me love

Let me love

Protected in the shadow of your wings

CELEBRATE

My heart sings

As my soul calls

"Come hear us play"

I want to hear my favorite songs

Gotta celebrate-Gotta celebrate

I'll have to drive all day

Gonna see the best band in the world

My heart sings

As a soul calls

"Come hear us play"

Just dropped by…

I'll dance a few

I can only stay a while

Let's hear something new

(Oh Lord, it looks like I'll be staying until two)

My heart sings

As my soul calls

"Hear us Play"

Let's hear another song

Feel the music flow

Let it lift your soul

Where else would I want to go

My heart sings

As a soul calls

"Listen to us play"

All the silver and the gold

Can never replace

The song in his heart

And a warm embrace

Who could ever forget the loving smile on his face

The Singer

He's a friend of mine

Dance to the rhythm

As he sings out the rhyme

31918

Love

Knows-

Love Knows-

How the heart Strengthens

And grows

Love knows where you'll be found

Love knows now

The beauty of a lifetime

With You

Love knows it's true

And Love Knows

he will find Himself

in You!

WITHOUT YOU

I want to hear your Voice
I want to be lost in your eyes
Lost in your touch-
Your lips upon mine
Won't you light your Red Lantern
For me-
Just for me
Brush the hair from my eyes
Sing me to sleep
I woke-up
From my deep dark Sleep
When I heard you Calling
Come to me please-
Kiss me-
Kiss me in life-
Kiss me in death-
I see them all...
And I know.
I am here without you

HUE

I hear you whisper as I sleep

You offer your hand

I pray you're offering it to me

I reach for you

And you retreat…

Just like you say, I always do;

I don't want to be alone

I've been alone for so long

I don't know what it's like to be

Fully loved

By a man

I've never been

I've spent my life

Chasing dreams

They turn to dust

In the palm of my hand

Blown away

By the wind…

MY BEAUTIFUL LUMBERJACK

It feels like
I saw him yesterday
He stood before me
Trying not to cry
Oblivious to my thoughts
Like a reflection of myself
I could see it in his eyes,
the pain
Telling me about his day
And how she lied.
Stripping him of any pride
That he, might still have left.
As his ten-year-old
Climbed the stairs,
Wildly bleached hair and adventurous eyes
A miniature of the man before me
But not broken
by the fight for-his own
The boy,

Curious and Eager

To be

Just like him…

Bright, Bold, and

In on our conversation

Which ceased,

When the boy stood by.

Later

Much later…

I got into my car

I leaned out and called to him

I told him..

"We really should go!"

He said, "Maybe…"

But I know,

His eyes said, Definitely, Maybe…

Like they always did,

As he said, "I'll call you later."

Like he always did.

I watched him

Open the gate for me

The one he had previously closed behind

It comes naturally

How he protects me

He's soft inside
And he protects
Without a thought
He has no one to protect him
Although I try...
I fall short,
Miserably short.
People think he's blind,
But his eyes are also mine...
We have our plans
But...
Life gets in the way
as it often does.
I wave back
and drive away.

So, whisper to me sweetly
Tell me it's not all the same
As you offer your hand
I pray you're offering it to me
When I reach for you
Promise-
Face to Face-

Promise-
You won't retreat-
And leave me
Standing alone
Again
In this miserable place.
This place
Where I face myself
With deep regret
Alone
Wondering if the soul lingers

Hoping for the familiar
or Searching
For something...
As if I expect him
to emerge from the house
Calling out
To me
As he sweetly smiles
Waving from the porch
So I can tell him again,

As he wraps his arms around me

How much I Love him

So, whisper to me sweetly

Tell me it's not all the same

As you offer your hand

I pray you're offering it to me

When I reach for you

Promise

J.K.

Help Me

Find a Rhyme

Purge the demons

Who haunt my soul

Won't you love me

Forevermore

I'll close my eyes

Promise me all that you can

And I'll believe it

Every single line

Even if you want to lie

Just because I can

Believe in you

Believing In me

Help Me

Find a Rhyme

Purge the demons

Who haunt my soul

Won't you love me

Forevermore

REAL MAN

Will you show me
What a real man is…
Of the earth
And I still don't know
What a real man is…
I've never been touched
By the hands of a real man…
I've never been loved
By the heart of a real man…
I've never been spoken to
With the words of a real man…
I've never been kissed
By the lips of a real man…
I've never seen myself
Through the eyes of a real man…
I've never had a real man
Put his body against mine…
Or pull mine to his.
Won't you take me by the hand
And show me
What a real man is…

WILL YOU

The rain poured
The thunder shook and rolled
I found myself in bed alone
Again...
Nothing new
Just ordinary
Instead of wondering who he was with
Again...
I was wondering who you were with
Again...
How did you get to me anyway
How did your voice;
Your words
Among a million others
Break free and travel to this place
A place within
Penetrating the pain and confusion
Resting upon my soul

Replacing hurt and fear
With the thought of you
Leaving me with a longing
To have you near
For you
To be here
Again...
Even if you only
Come
By way of dream
Again...
If I close my eyes
Will you
Come...
Again

and again
and again...

THE EXTRAORDINARY LITERARY

Dance with me

Just once

Before I die

I want to know

How it feels

To be

With one set free

In the arms of a man

In whom

His Creator can be seen

Take me

Into your arms

Envelope me in His love

In your Love

In Freedom

Teach me to see

Dance with me

Just once

Before I die

Let me know
The love of a man
The touch of a man
Not afraid

Not afraid
Yet willing to crawl
Not afraid
To face a fall

A man willing to fall
To his knees
And whisper prayers
Of Love and sweet release

Dance with me
Just once
Before I die

TOO FAR DOWN

Sleek and slow
With nowhere to go

Wondering how...
You see it that way

I am just being
Who I am

It's too far down
To be up here all alone

Wondering how...
How
I came on too strong

I won't breakdown
Because
I'm not going to back down

This time
Around

I am just being
Who I am

Sleek and slow
With nowhere to go

Wondering how...
I came on too strong

Wondering how...
You see it that way

It's too far down
To be walking
All alone

I am just being
Who I am

Sleek and slow

With nowhere to go

Wondering how...
I came on too strong

Wondering how...
You see it that way

It's too far down
To be walking
All alone

Baby won't you take me home

SAVE ME

Sitting here dreaming
I use to see you in my dreams
I use to feel you when I closed my eyes

Sitting here dreaming
The noise clouds my mind
I try focusing on you

I can't see you anymore
I can't dream you anymore
I can't feel you anymore

Why run away
Run with me Baby
Run with me Baby
Run with me Baby

Sitting here dreaming
Save me from myself
Save me from a lifetime of loneliness

I can't see you anymore

I can't dream you anymore

I can't feel you anymore

Run with me

Run with me Baby

Run with me Baby

Run with me Baby

I can't see you anymore

I can't dream you anymore

I can't feel you anymore

I can't see you anymore

I can't dream you anymore

I can't feel you anymore

Save Me

PARAPRAXIS

Freudian slip

Meets

Freudian slip

Head on collision

When he was looking

The other way.

He played me good

The chemistry was hot

Pulling me in…

Leading me on…

"Believe in a future"

That's what I want…

When in his mind I am only…

Meant to be…

Cuisine for a night

Freudian slip

Meets

Freudian slip

Mine in response

To his…

Slip of the tongue

Wandering of the mind

A touch of jealousy

Blinding communication
Both of us
Living in fear
That history will repeat
While he was slipping the tongue
I was...
Leading his response
Half of the time
Holding on to me
The other changing his mind
Not letting go of what he has
isn't much...
Wanting me to do the same
I'm sick of playing
Petty games
Excuse me
For avoiding
The pain
The unnecessary pain
Caused by a stupid---

Freudian slip
I'll sit home
And
Eat alone

Frozen

Fettuccine

Once again

Instead…

Of being loved

And dream

of a better tomorrow…

Forgetting

The past

And the stupid---

Freudian slip

Meets

Freudian slip

Head on collision

How 'bout

A love that will last

TO BE SEEN AND NOT HEARD

To be Seen and Not Heard

Be as silent as you want to be

I can feel you there

Just like you are laying there

Next to me

But silence for now

Is not for me…

Even if your words are not meant for me

I still want to dream…

I spent too many years in the darkness

A different silence

Too many years

In a lost city

The city of despair

I want to speak

Until I lose my voice

Or when my heart dies.

I only want to be silent again

When I'm in your arms

The arms of a friend

When I finally know

That you really care

I'll be silent

In your arms

I dream...

You hide me away

From the darkness

From the city of despair

Take me further away

From this lost city

Take me somewhere...

A place for just you with me

Take me there

From the darkness into the light

Away from the nightmare

Away from the settled for

To a place...

The place

Where neither of us need to speak

To be heard and not seen

THE LINE

We didn't take

The easy way out

The line wasn't crossed…

We went back

We are where we began

We can still hold hands

The kiss

Forgotten

We remain

friends

It makes me wonder

Why…

When it would have been

So much easier to forget

Our troubles

Instead.

THE DEVIL'S DANCE

I've been dancing with the devil. I fear.

I found what I need to appease...the emptiness

To feed the hunger...

Not exactly what I'm craving

Not what I truly desire...

But enough to fill...the emptiness

And to keep it still

For a time.

He even looks

Something like

What I'm craving...

Though I know; they'd never taste the same.

And I think I have it;

All figured out.

I think I can;

Work it this way.

Minimizing the loneliness

Which works

For us...

It's frightening...

The ease in which we

Balance our souls

On the line

The thin line

Closer to the edge;

Than not.

Elevated above the world

We've come to know.

On the edge…

Is it

The edge of damnation

Or

Do we have further

To go…

A false move…

Do we lose our soul?

I think I can

I think I know

I think it will be okay

Even if

We become

Two-Too

Involved.

We didn't ask

We didn't know

What we said;

When we said

I do

To...

Them

We didn't know

We'd get this.

We didn't know

Forever

With him

With her

Would be...

Like this.

That it would,

Set us

Into chains of misery

And loneliness.

I think it's the edge of despair

Not the edge of destruction

Or

Damnation.

Is it a sin

To let go.

To fall from the ledge

Into the arms

Of one

With the same

Affliction

And cure each other.

With the touch

Of flesh

To Flesh.

Is it selfish

Is it a sin

To want

To need

To fulfill

Not just a desire;

But an emptiness

Within..

Is it a sin…

It probably is…

And then I think

It might not be…

Isn't it a sin

For them to be

Him with her

And

Her with him

or was it

Her with her

and

Him and him..

And we

Alone

Again...
Will we sit
On that damned couch
And watch that B movie...
Not even holding hands
Pretending we can only be friends
Each knowing
That if we do
Get close enough
Again;
Touch again

And accidently
Kiss...
Again...
We can't stop
We won't stop.
We're both starving
And we are each other's
Answer
To satisfy...
The aching...
The craving...
And we are each other's
Cure.
Is it a sin

Have I been dancing with the devil

Can he steal my soul

If I won't give it?

Can I keep it safe...

Even though we may give in...

This time.

MUG SHOTS AND FINGERPRINTS

Mug shots

And

Fingerprints

Taken by a man

I could surely kiss

Baby won't you

Hold my hand

Just a little

Longer-----

A man with taste

In expensive shoes

Fragrance from a dream

Diagramming

And

Recording my tattoos with ease

One of which

Is

Attributed

To you

Forever this moment

Preserved in time.

Hanging from the cord

Around my neck
Credentials
Swing across my chest
The proof
Of this moment
Is in the smile.
Mug Shots
And
Fingerprints
A beautiful dream
Quickly extinguished
By his wedding ring
Mug shots
And
Fingerprints
Taken by a man
I surely can't kiss
You can understand
But he is forever welcome
To hold my hand

ALL IN ALL

You think you understand me

You haven't a clue

Go ahead and condemn me

There is nothing I need from you

You think you understand me

You haven't a clue

All I want

I could never have

What I wanted

Was you

But that's not news

To anyone

Except for you

All I want

I could never have

And that's all I wanted from you

ULTIMATE

Bravo! Bravo!
Funny how
The bullies
Have to be heard...
How they
Have to
Let you know
You're within
Their grasp
They deliver
Their words
To prove
To you
They can
Move past
Your lines
Your lines
Of
Love
All that they think you've drawn
And
If you don't
Comply

They'll erase what you love

And

Take it away

And

All that you own.

How absurd

You think me a fool

Nestled down

For a long winter's nap

Ready to step aside

For

Love

And

You wake me

For what

To tell me

You're

Afraid

I'll draw first-blood

I don't draw first-blood

I leave that up to you

Whatever happened to…

Good old fashion ground rules

I know

What I love

And

I love

What I do

And

I know

What I've earned

And

I know

What I'd do

For love...

My lines clearly defined

Sculpted so you'd know

When you're

Holding the knife to his throat

Another needle to his arm

Crossing my lines of love

Will only bring you down

Bravo! Bravo!

WAR

Why do we fight

Why do we make war

To settle a score?

A losing battle from the start

If everyone would stop

To

Count the cost

Most war

Would never have begun

War

Would never have had

a

Start

Screaming for peace

Yet making more

War

Because

Someone whispered,

"We have to settle a score?"

No Modus Operandi

Roisin Rzeznik

LOVE

No silence; just thought
A string of prayers
A note of innocence
This thread of hope
You've given me

Unconscious motivation
A longing for your touch
A desperate prayer
Then I heard
"Let me guide you, Darling and beware"

Now, I thought I was out here
On this road all alone
Lost and broken
A destination unknown
Then I heard
"Let me guide you, Darling and beware"

I wanted to believe
He never meant to hurt me
He never meant to cause me pain
I was drowning in my tears
When I heard you

Call my name

Now, I thought I was out here
Lost on this road all alone
Left to forever roam
I had to take the chance

Through the darkness
You were my light
My heart overflowing with thoughts of you
You brought me to my knees

You carried me through the dark of night
Better than any star
I could feel you there
My guiding light
You brought me to my knees
I knew then
You're all I ever need
You are all I'll ever need

You're everything to me
Better than any star
More than the rest
By far
My guiding light

Roisin Rzeznik

Carrying me through

I reach for you

Not knowing if it will fade or endure

No silence; just love

A string of prayers

A note of innocence

This thread of love

You've given me

I know

You're all I ever need

You are everything to me

You are all I'll ever need

I've gotta take the chance

Tell me we can make it last

You're all I'll ever need

Love, you are all I'll ever need

TIME

He shined so bright for a time
Then he lost
The girl and the rhyme
Rhyme for me
Baby rhyme for me
I'll ask you
Baby rhyme for me
One more time
I'll tell you; He shined
He shined so bright
Then he lost
The girl and the rhyme
Once again
Like a child I see
I see you in my mind
We're like children; You and me
"Come play with me!"
Baby will you rhyme with me
Before we run out of time
Let's make the world one big rhyme
You and me

EARLY BIRD...

Like an illusion---
Always in sight
And
Always just out of reach
Unable to be grasped
What makes me complete
I wonder if you feel like me
Or
Do I feel like you
I feel like
I'm only doing time here
I'm a last resort
When they've drained
Every other resource...
Then maybe
To them
And I hope not to you...
I'm just like that smoke
They're out to bum
"Hey, Babe, you mind if I hit you up for some?"
Thoughts for a Friend

COFFEE

What you missed

When the door closed

He pressed her gently up against the door

Kissing her deeply

Part passion

Part pity

His lips lightly caressed her face

As they moved to her neck…

Overwhelmed by affection

Her strength drained

through

To the floor boards

Every muscle gave at once

Breathless

She looked up at the ceiling and whispered

"Dear God"

Her eyes closed tight
As she felt her back
Slide down the door
Collapsing in a heap
At his feet
He scooped her up into his arms
As she caught her breath
Her eyes opened again…
And he continued to hold her in his arms…
The door opened
And they reemerged…

CHICAGO

There is a man
A friend
One I hope to find
Walking by my side
At least for a moment
A moment of sweet serenity
A moment to know me
Sunsets and ocean tides
Take my hand
I thought you were the one
To make me come alive
Open your eyes
To your own heart
Take my hand
Show me what it's like
To love
For a moment
Run with me
Teach me to love

Beyond what we know
Navigate us through

Just me and you
All the promises
And the dreams
Navigate us through
Beyond what we know
Sunsets and ocean tides
Let's make our own memories
Forget the disguise
Release your grasp
On reality
Toss the pride
Take my hand
Teach me to love
Beyond what we know
I know you are the one
To make me come alive
In Chicago
Today I see
I see today

Two days
Of wandering aimlessly
Through a maze of indifference
Through crowds of people
Past the chill of their hearts
I know you have the answers

And I know I'll be wandering

Alone

Once again

Through the crowds

Crowds that don't notice

Crowds that don't see

Me

Wandering aimlessly

Past dawn

Through empty city streets

Of Chicago

Wishing-hoping-dreaming

You'd be there with me

Hand in hand

Loving beyond

What we know

Wandering alone

Once again

Always

Wandering alone

Will I ever know...

That moment of sweet serenity

As you look me in the eyes

Taking my hand

As we wander

Through the city streets

Knowing what we know

In that moment of sweet release

As we wander

Through the city streets

Of Chicago

When I ask you to never wake me

Knowing what we know

In that moment of sweet surrender

Knowing what we know

Wandering

Alone

Chicago